Paper Tiger
An imprint of Dragon's World
Dragon's World Ltd, Limpsfield, Surrey, RH8 0DY, Great Britain

First published by Dragon's World Ltd 1994

© Dragon's World Ltd 1994
© Illustrations: Rodney Matthews 1994

All the illustrations in this miniature edition are from *In Search of
Forever* by Rodney Matthews published by Dragon's World Ltd

The catalogue record for this book is available from the British
Library

ISBN 1 85028 271 4

Editor: Julie Davis
Designer: Megra Mitchell
Art Director: John Strange
Editorial Director: Pippa Rubinstein

Printed in Hong Kong

RODNEY MATTHEWS

PAPER TIGER MINIATURES

The beauty of Fantasy is that anything is possible. The iron laws that govern earthly existence are suspended and what appears often seems more real in a way, more as it should be, than its equivalent in our world.

Fantasy worlds reflect our own. They are glimpses of parallel universes which have unfolded along different lines but are influenced by what happens in our own dimension. Ideas flit across the divide, emerging changed but recognizable in their new settings.

DRUMBOOGIE
Inks 70 x 100 cm

As in dreams, our wishes articulate themselves on a grand scale; but so do our

fears, and in the struggle between them our everyday strife is acted out on a heroic level.

No Mean City Inks 50 x 100 cm

There is, too, the thrill of exploration. In a world with few remaining natural wonders that we are not familiar with through film, imaginative art opens up fresh feasts of possibility.

THE TWILIGHT TOWER
Inks and gouache 100 x 70 cm

Life often feels like a game we are playing by rules which have not been fully explained, and which are anyway subject to periodic change without warning. In Fantasy this is often exactly the case.

THE CHEQUERED FLOOR
Inks 36 x 26 cm

And with these practicalities lifted it is not just the decor that can be changed to suit one's taste. The morbid poet, for instance, need not content himself with a skull on the desk but can transform his whole abode into one planted in the desert.

WERTHER'S SKULL
Inks 36 x 52 cm

It is not just wishes and fears that breed in the imagination. Many other strange fancies doggedly persist there long after their dismissal from the waking world because in some irrational way they do still make sense.

Things bizarre have a certain attraction even when one would not like to meet them at first hand. Rock musicians throughout the multiverse, however, always tend to go over the top.

Encore at the End of Time
Inks 70 x 100 cm

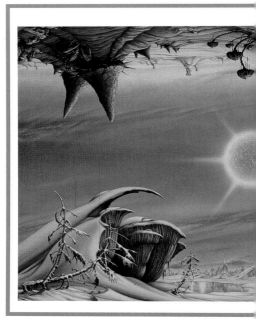

Fantasy illustrations may seem totally surreal when divorced from the stories that gave rise to them, but they have a curious ability to stand alone with no more explanation than our fancy cares.

INVERTED LANDSCAPES
Inks 70 x 100 cm

Often it feels preferable to hang on to the enigma. We may wonder what reasons the characters have for being where they are, what is going through their minds and whether they are leaving or heading towards that stronghold in the distance, but we do not really want to be told.

ESTCARP ONE
Inks and gouache 37 x 48 cm

Alternatve and fascinating modes of transport are not the least of the attractions of other worlds ...

IN THE FLAMELANDS
Inks

SKELLNAG'S PROMISE Inks and gouache 50 x 100 cm

.... though some are more obviously useful in a tight corner than others.

What a difference wings
make to a journey!

A View over Isengard
Inks 50 x 100 cm

In crowded worlds everyone wants to escape the city. In empty ones it's the opposite.

Some cities are more than just homes to large numbers of people, they have also the mystical aura of a Grail Castle or New Jerusalem and so finding them is as much a spiritual quest as a physical adventure.

TANELORN
Inks and gouache 70 x 100 cm

But however proud and mighty they are in their prime, all stone cities fall to nature in the fullness of time.

MIRADOR
Inks 60 x 100 cm

However, in Fantasy there are always fresh places and people to find, new challenges to face and perils to be overcome.

THE ICE SPIRIT
Inks and gouache 70 x 100 cm

The contest between good and evil or order and chaos forever throws up novel permutations and strange new protagonists. And whenever one side seems decisively victorious it is never really so. Some germ of the vanquished survives to start the contest over again.

THE PREDATOR
Inks 32 x 64 cm

In everyone's heart lies an image of some place of final rest and fulfilment, a place removed from the buffetings of life but forever beyond reach, always just over the next mountain range or perhaps the one after that.

CHASE THE DRAGON
INKS 40 x 40 CM

Such visions lure us
through life and
shape its pattern.
Over and over we
believe we have reached the place

only to discover it is just another way-station. Only in Fantasy and the human heart do such places truly exist and their attainment is as rare as they are wonderful. SANCTUARY Inks 60 x 100 cm